Preface

by James Warren
Socialist Workers Party 1988 candidate for president of the United States

Since we launched our election campaign in March, my running mate, Kathleen Mickells, and I have been raising the proposals that are in this pamphlet, "An Action Program to Confront the Coming Economic Crisis." This program, first discussed by the SWP leadership in the weeks following the October 1987 stock market crash, was adopted by the party's National Committee in June 1988.

During the SWP election campaign we've reached hundreds of thousands of people through newspaper coverage and radio and television interviews, as well as through scores of meetings and discussions. And everywhere we've gone — whether it's London, England, or St. George's, Grenada; Paris, France, or Panama City, Panama; Atlanta, Georgia, or Auckland, New Zealand; New York City or Arusha, Tanzania; Sydney, Australia, or Managua, Nicaragua; Montreal, Quebec, or Price, Utah — we've found that these proposals are listened to carefully and taken seriously.

In discussions with workers at meetings and plant gates and with farmers, students, and others, we find that there is growing awareness since the October stock market crash that promises of economic stability have no foundation and that a devastating depression is in the offing. Even people who are not necessarily in agreement with us sense that we are addressing key questions facing working people today.

There are tens of thousands of workers who are looking for the perspectives presented in this program. Kathleen and I and all of our supporters will be joining in the effort to sell as many pamphlets as we can and to discuss this program at every available opportunity. Workers and others who agree with it will want to carry copies with them to sell to those they get into discussions with about what working people can do in the face of the coming economic and social disaster.

In thinking about how to discuss the action program, I've found it useful to refer to two columns in the socialist newsweekly the *Militant* written by its editor Doug Jenness, who is also the Socialist Workers Party's 1988 presidential campaign manager. The columns deal with the international fight for a shorter workweek both in the past and today. These articles appear as the concluding item in this pamphlet.

A necessary step in fighting for this action program today is to involve more and more people in the discussion of it, winning as many of them as possible to support its perspectives. In the course of this process — which will extend well beyond the present election campaign — many will be convinced to join the fight for a workers' and farmers' government and to become members of the Socialist Workers Party.

July 2, 1988

An Action Program to Confront the Coming Economic Crisis

Presented by the National Committee of the Socialist Workers Party

I. CAPITALIST PROSPECTS IN THE COMING DECADE

On October 19, 1987, prices on the New York Stock Exchange plunged more than at any time in this century; more steeply than the October 1929 Wall Street crash that signaled the Great Depression of the 1930s. Every working person feels more uneasy today as a result. And with good reason.

The crash rapidly spread to every other stock market around the world. It revealed the explosive pressures that have been accumulating in the capitalist world system for nearly two decades.

These pressures have accelerated in the 1980s. Their consequences can already be seen in the devastation faced by the most impoverished layers of working people and the poorest regions of the world: millions of families without homes; crumbling roads, bridges, hospitals, and schools; working-class neighborhoods with disintegrating sanitation and public health services; growing numbers of youth denied jobs; and moves aimed at restricting democratic rights.

This creeping social crisis points to the coming reality that a vast majority of working people around the world are going to confront.

World depression inevitable

We face the inevitability of a world depression that will usher in an economic and social crisis engulfing working people in every part of the world the capitalist market reaches. Any new partial economic crisis — a sharp recession,a series of major crop failures, an explosion of inflation, stock-market crashes, or banking and debt disasters — can precipitate this depression.

Hundreds of millions more will join the already enormous ranks of those out of work and with no way to make a living in the countryside or city. The devastating plague of mass unemployment and underemployment will not only worsen throughout Asia, Africa, Latin America, and the Pacific. In those imperialist countries that have prospered the most since World War II, joblessness and impoverishment will hit with a degree of force not felt since the 1930s. Depression conditions throughout the capitalist world will accelerate the growing social, economic, and political crisis in Eastern Europe and the Soviet Union.

More farmers will be driven off the land. Small businesses will be ruined. Homelessness will increase, and soup kitchen lines will grow. The breakdowns we are already seeing in our roads, bridges, and mass transportation; the decline in health care and education; the increasing destruction of the earth's forests, soil, atmosphere, rivers, and oceans — all will get much worse. Inflationary bursts will be all the more devastating as we pay for the capitalists' international orgy of money creation, borrowing, and speculation.

Life will become even more brutal for those workers who face racial discrimination in the job market, education, and housing. The employers will attempt to drive back the gains of women in their fight for equality in hiring, on the job, and throughout society, as well as in their struggle for access to full knowledge about reproduction and birth control and the right to safe, legal abortions.

As workers around the world organize and fight more effectively to defend ourselves against these mounting attacks, the rulers will increasingly turn to more brutal methods. The police and armed forces will be called in against our strikes and demonstrations more often. War and the threat of war will become more common. Reactionary political movements will grow, aimed at dividing working people from each other and from our allies and ultimately at crushing our resistance.

Workers and farmers need to recognize what capitalism holds in store for us, and what our organizations must do to defend ourselves against the devastating effects of this social catastrophe that is impending. To prepare for tomorrow, however, we need to understand the conditions faced by working people worldwide today.

II. WORKING PEOPLE IN THE SEMICOLONIAL WORLD

In Africa, Asia, and Latin America millions of peasants are being driven off their land, joining millions of other working people without jobs. Untold numbers of workers have little or no shelter. Malnutrition, hunger, and disease are increasing. Hundreds of millions are less and less able to afford the goods that they want and need, either those produced at home or those imported. Millions of acres of farm and forest land are being raped by companies from imperialist countries seeking to make a quick profit. Their "development" projects are destroying domestic food production, stripping small farmers of their land, and ruining the natural environment of these oppressed nations.

Imperialist oppression

These are the social consequences of the superexploitation and domination of the semicolonial countries by the ruling capitalist families in the imperialist countries. These families use their vast economic power — organized through the major banks and international monetary agencies that front for these banks — and their political and military clout to impose unequal trade relations on the semicolonial countries. Sellers in the oppressed nations get declining prices for their products on the world market, while buyers in these countries must pay rising prices for manufactured goods and technology purchased from companies owned by the ruling rich in the economically advanced capitalist countries. The semicolonial countries must export more and more of the goods produced from their soil and with the labor of their working people in order to buy the same tractor, truck, or other piece of imported equipment. Economic development that can lead to broad industrialization and a rising standard of living for toilers in the semicolonial world is blocked off. Previously touted "economic miracles" like those in Brazil and Mexico are collapsing.

These disparities in trade are reproduced and reinforced through quotas and tariffs, dumping of goods on the world market that undercut sales of products from semicolonial countries, and a mass of nontariff trade barriers. The United Nations Conference on Trade and Development, for example, has identified some 700 such unfair nontariff practices — ranging from government subsidies, to health and technical standards, to deliberately complex administrative measures — designed to increase the profits of the wealthy families in the imperialist countries to the detriment of the nations peopled by the majority of humanity.

These trade barriers are not imposed equally. They are applied differentially in a system of punishment and reward in order to blackmail governments in the semicolonial world.

We are all in the debt trap

As profit rates in industry have declined, the ruling families of the imperialist countries, through their banks, have put more and more of their capital into an international loan-sharking operation preying on the workers and peasants in the semicolonial world. Governments in Africa, Latin America, the Caribbean, Asia, and the Pacific have borrowed heavily from banks in New York, Tokyo, Paris, London, Stockholm, Sydney, Toronto, and other financial centers.

Altogether the foreign debt of these oppressed countries is $1.2 trillion! In Latin America and the Caribbean alone, the total foreign debt at the end of 1987 was $410 billion. In Africa the debt stands at $218 billion.

Acting for the wealthiest capitalists, the big banks suck billions of dollars in interest payments out of these countries every year. In 1986, for example, Latin America and the Caribbean alone transferred more than $22 billion in interest payments to the coffers of Chase Manhattan, the Royal Bank of Canada, Barclay's, Sumitomo, Credit Lyonnais, and other imperialist banks. Institutions such as the International Monetary Fund, World Bank, and Inter-American Development Bank — the latter two supposedly set up to help the developing countries — are at the hub of this brutal rip-off.

To keep these interest payments flowing in, the imperialist bankers demand that governments in the oppressed countries cut wages and increase speedup, slash even minimal social expenditures, and implement other brutal austerity measures aimed at squeezing more and more out of working people. The bankers demand that these countries turn over ownership of even more of their soil, forests, mines, and industries to imperialist interests. More and more of the economy's production is pushed toward the export trade to gain foreign exchange in order "to pay the debt," instead of producing the food, clothes, and other basic goods needed by workers and peasants at home.

In growing numbers of these countries, income from export sales has been insufficient to make even the interest payments or pay back part of the original loan, let alone to use for economic development. Consequently they've been forced to borrow more money just to pay the mounting interest on the existing debt.

The entire relationship becomes a vicious trap. It's similar to what happens to working farmers in the United States who can't make enough income from sales of their products to cover costs, so they become debt slaves to the banks.

The foreign debt of the semicolonial countries is simply unpayable. As it spirals ever higher, it can lead only to one end: massive bank failures that will trigger a world economic disaster. And as the bubbles burst, working people everywhere will suffer the devastating consequences.

Labor organizations throughout Latin America and the Caribbean have organized demonstrations and held conferences to raise the just demand for cancellation of this foreign debt.

In May 1987 representatives of fifty-six union organizations from twenty-five countries met in Brazil for a Latin American and Caribbean Trade Union Conference on the Foreign Debt. Delegates called for cancellation of the debt and for an international campaign to expose the effects of the debt burden on their countries. They issued an appeal for "the solidarity of the workers of the industrialized countries, through their trade union federations, with the campaign against the payment of the foreign debt."

A similar conference took place in June 1987 in Trinidad and Tobago. The Fifth Trade Union Conference on Unity and Solidarity of the Caribbean Workers urged repudiation of the foreign debt and condemned unequal terms of trade, tariffs, quotas, and other barriers to economic development imposed on the Caribbean and Latin America.

In December 1987 representatives of twenty-six trade unions in Africa met in Addis Ababa, Ethiopia, to discuss the foreign debt and its consequences for working people. They issued a declaration urging all governments and mass organizations in Africa to "unite their forces with the aim of achieving the cancellation or the collective repudiation of the debt."

The government of Cuba initiated the call for canceling the debt. More than any other government it has helped give voice to this demand by working people in the oppressed nations. As Cuban President Fidel Castro has explained, the debt is economically unpayable, politically uncollectible, and morally indefensible. That must become the motto of workers the world over — for the sake of justice and for our own self-interest.

III. THE WORKING CLASS IN THE UNITED STATES

The catastrophe that workers in the semicolonial world are already suffering is not remote from U.S. shores. This devastation has already hit millions of workers in the United States, foreshadowing what the future holds.

Many of us already have a lurking sense of insecurity, a reflection of the fact that no worker is guaranteed a job in capitalist society. There is no such thing as a permanent job. We are all temporary workers.

All of us depend on being able to sell our labor power in order to feed, clothe, and shelter ourselves and our families. The big majority of us have no access to land to grow food, nor do we have any possibility of going into business for ourselves. Without a job, we don't have any way to make ends meet and maintain a standard of living fit for human beings.

A creeping social crisis

Washington is crowing that the official jobless rate was 5.6 percent in May 1988, a drop from more than 10 percent in 1982 at the peak of the last recession. But 5.6 percent unemployment represents almost *seven million* workers and affects tens of millions more when their families are included. Joblessness today is higher than most years between 1941 and 1975.

Moreover, millions are not counted in official government unemployment figures. These include young workers who have never been able to get a job, workers whose unemployment compensation has run out, undocumented workers who do not report to unemployment offices out of fear of being deported, women who haven't been working but want a job, and farmers driven off their land and forced to seek wage jobs for the first time.

A growing number of us with jobs are denied real full-time employment. Fifteen percent of the officially employed in 1986 worked less than half the year. Another twenty million workers in the United States are forced to work part-time jobs that average only twenty-two-hours' pay a week.

The result has been the pauperization of a growing layer of workers in the United States. Since 1980 the percentage of the U.S. population living at or below the poverty line has averaged more than 14 percent, up from an average of 11.7 percent over the previous seven years. Forty percent of the 118 million holding jobs in 1987 earned less than $11,000 a year.

The free-market "prosperity" trumpeted in the big-business media is a myth for many working people. While the average per capita income among the wealthiest one-fifth of the population grew from $70,260 in 1979 to $76,300 in 1986, it *declined* — from $8,761 to $8,033 — among the one-fifth of the population with the lowest income.

The dimensions of the creeping economic and social crisis in the United States can no longer be hidden as it affects more and more of us. Millions of working people, many of them families pushed out of their homes, are now living on street corners, in bus stations, or in cars. Public health care has deteriorated. Preventable diseases like tuberculosis are on the rise. More than 30,000 people have died from Acquired Immune Deficiency Syndrome (AIDS), while government aid to the victims of this deadly disease has been totally inadequate. Breakdowns and disasters in mass transportation are becoming more, not less, common. Nuclear and other poisonous wastes proliferate in our air, soil, and water. We're more than twice as likely to be in a state or federal prison today as we were fifteen years ago; nearly 100 people have been put to death since 1976, overwhelmingly working people; and nearly 2,000 more of us are on death row today.

Devastation of workers who are Black

Hardest hit by the crisis are those of us who are victims of discrimination because of our skin color, national origin, or language: Blacks, Chicanos, Puerto Ricans, Asian-Americans, and immigrants from Central and South America, the Caribbean, Asia, the Pacific, and elsewhere.

Let's take a look at the conditions already confronting working-class communities that are Black, since this offers a preview of what capitalism has in store for wider and wider layers of our class.

While overall official unemployment is 5.6 percent, it is more than 12 percent among workers who are Black. And nearly 35 percent among young people who are Black.

In the Midwest, much of which has been traumatized by plant shutdowns and farm foreclosures, unemployment of Black workers has averaged more than 23 percent throughout the 1980s. In the city of Milwaukee it is 27 percent right now.

Measured by 1986 dollars, 14 percent of Black families now live on less than $5,000 a year, as compared to 8.9 percent in 1978. Thirty percent of all Black families live on less than $10,000, an increase from 27.4 percent in 1978.

The real picture of the disaster striking Black working-class communities has been hidden through distorted statistics aimed at covering up this growing inequality. This is done by lumping together the incomes and general living conditions of Blacks who are workers with the figures for the small minority of Blacks who are in the middle class.

Today the best-off one-fifth of Black families receive 47.4 percent of the total income of all Blacks, while the poorest one-fifth receive 3.4 percent. Averaging income and other statistics together for these two layers of the Black population disguises the brutality of the economic pressures bearing down on the big majority who are workers.

From 1978 to 1986, the percent of Black families with annual incomes over $50,000 increased by 14 percent. But the percent of Black families trying to get by on less than $5,000 a year increased by 57 percent.

The same pattern can be seen in housing. While a small minority of Blacks have moved into integrated — often middle-class — neighborhoods, most workers who are Black remain trapped in neighborhoods that are as segregated as they were twenty years ago. And segregated housing means segregated schools with fewer resources and inadequate educational facilities. This results in inferior elementary and high school education for the children of working-class families that are Black and fewer opportunities for ongoing education.

The percentage of Blacks attending schools with a predominantly Black and Latino student body was 77 percent in 1968 and dropped to 64 percent in 1972. But the figure has remained roughly the same ever since.

And school segregation has increased during the 1980s in some states, such as New York, where 57 percent of Black students attend schools that are 90 to 100 percent Black and Latino. More than 80 percent of the Black students in the states of New York, Illinois, and Michigan go to schools that are more than half Black or Latino in composition.

Little wonder then that since 1976 the percent of Afro-American high school graduates starting college has declined from 34 percent to 26 percent.

The number of working-class families in which a woman is the sole income-earner has risen rapidly and among Black families has soared from 25 percent in 1965 to 42 percent in 1986. The combined race and sex discrimination faced by these workers, along with utterly inadequate public child care and other social services, has resulted in a median income for these families of $7,999.

The severity of the crisis for working-class families whose breadwinners are Black is intensified by the sharp decline in government aid. While the buying power of aid to dependent children and food stamps rose during the 1960s and early 1970s, it has fallen since. In 1984 it was 22 percent lower than in 1972 and had fallen almost to its level at the end of the 1950s.

Joblessness, government slashing of health services, and malnutrition literally spell death for workers who are Black. In some of the most impoverished working-class communities that are Black, infant mortality rates have gone up. In Central Harlem, the rate reached 27.6 per 1,000 live births by the end of 1986, a 73 percent increase since 1984. This is double the rate of 13.6 in Cuba, a country with far fewer resources. Nationally the infant mortality rate for Blacks is about 18 per 1,000 live births, compared to 10.6 for the population as a whole.

Tuberculosis, a disease that had virtually been wiped out in the United States, rose in New York City from 17 cases per 100,000 residents in 1978 to 31.4 per 100,000 in 1986 — that is, 83 percent.

Black men contract TB at nine times the citywide average.

This past year in the United States an estimated 3,000 babies were born infected with AIDS. Babies who are Black are 25 more times likely to inherit this virus than babies who are white. Nationally, Blacks constitute 12 percent of the total population, but 25 percent of the people who have developed AIDS. This higher susceptibility to this deadly disease, for which there is currently no known cure, is directly attributable to poverty levels flowing from decades of forms of segregation.

Growing inequality in the work force

The devastation of Black working-class families has widened the gap between their average economic and social conditions and those of the working class as a whole. This gap had begun to narrow following the civil rights victories that were won in the 1960s and that were advanced in the beginning of the 1970s.

The big majority of workers who are unemployed or living below the poverty level are white, but workers who are Black make up a disproportionate number of those who have been driven into these conditions in recent years. In the 1980s a worker who is Black is more than twice as likely to be jobless as any other worker, a bigger gap than most years since World War II. The number of working-class families living on less than $5,000 has gone up by 39 percent since 1975; however, the number of Black families in this category has jumped by 60 percent. The median income of Black families is 60 percent that of families as a whole in the United States, down from 63 percent in the early 1970s. Today the mortality rate for infants who are Black is more than 70 percent higher than for all babies born in the United States, up from between 60 and 65 percent in the early 1970s.

Under capitalism the life of a worker is simply worth less, and that of a worker who is not white, still less. This is even codified by the courts and prison system. Prosecutors demand the death penalty in 49 percent of the capital murder cases where a Black is accused of killing a white, compared to 11 percent of the cases where a Black is charged with killing another Black.

The devastation of working-class communities that are Black over the last decade is the product of the workings of capitalism in a society with a legacy of racial discrimination. Combined with the growing class differentiation within the Black population, the result for workers who are Black has been less desegregation and more resegregation — in the job market, in the schools, and in housing.

This is a blow to the lives and living standards of all workers.

Gains such as desegregation of schools and housing, securing political rights, unionization of workers who are Black, advancing Blacks into jobs once reserved for whites only, raising the minimum wage — all these laid the ground to improve the wages, working conditions, education, and living standards of all working people.

Most importantly, the victory over Jim Crow segregation by the civil rights struggles of the 1950s and 1960s strengthened the entire working class politically, and the rulers have not been able to roll back this historic conquest. The advances in the rights of workers who are Black promote greater unification of our ranks in the face of the racial and other divisions imposed by capitalism. These gains aid workers, regardless of nationality or sex, in seeing that we are all part of one class; this understanding helps to undermine the effects of individual competition for jobs and security that the employers use to pit us against one another and increase our exploitation.

The same is true for overcoming the divisions imposed by the capitalists to block unity with other workers targeted for discrimination because of their skin color, language, or national origin. Chicanos, Puerto Ricans, and Asian-Americans face many forms of special oppression in employment and education, on the job, from the cops and courts, and throughout society. Workers who are American Indians live and work under some of the worst conditions in the United States. Many workers who are recent immigrants to the United States face the added discrimination meted out to noncitizens. The employers seek to keep immigrant workers in the pariah status of "illegals" and "aliens." The aim is to superexploit the labor of these foreign-born workers, paying them subminimum wages, enforcing inhuman working conditions, refusing them basic social services — and trying to deny them even the hope of economic and social advancement.

Segregation of women in the work force

The employers also seek to promote divisions between workers who are male and those who are female. Over the past five decades, tens of millions of women in the United States have poured into the work force at an accelerating rate. Especially following the rise of struggles for equal rights in the 1970s, a vanguard layer of working women battled their way into jobs previously held almost solely by men. These include unionized industrial jobs in coal mining, steel, oil refineries, auto assembly lines, and construction.

Despite these gains, sex segregation in the workplace remains a massive barrier both to women's equality and to working-class unity. Today half of all women and 70 percent of all men still work in jobs where at least 80 percent of their coworkers are of the same sex.

Layoffs during the 1981-82 recession cut into some of the gains won by women in getting industrial union jobs, and the much deeper downturns ahead will lead to sharper attacks on women's equality in employment and job opportunities.

The majority of workers who are women, including millions of heads of households, work at jobs for minimum wage or close to it. Millions of other women who are single parents with small children are forced to live on welfare and federal aid to families with dependent children. This is not because these women don't want to work, but because they are unable to find jobs and affordable child-care facilities. Growing demoralization and declining self-confidence among many of these women is a direct result of these conditions.

Women struggling to survive and raise families on their own have always constituted a high percentage of the most impoverished layer of the working class. Today their numbers are growing. High unemployment and declining real wages have intensified pressures on the working class, increasing the breakup of larger family units. At the same time, women have become less willing to accept a lifetime of economic dependence and subordination, whatever difficulties the alternative entails.

Breaking down sex barriers in employment and the workplace undermines prejudice against women and narrows one of the fundamental divisions used by the capitalists to weaken our class. As long as working-class women remain confined to the narrow world of the home, dependent economically on a man, it is much more difficult for them to engage in political activity and struggles to defend their class interests.

The influx of millions of women into the work force has brought them into social and political life in a qualitatively new way, increasing their self-confidence and fighting capacities to the benefit of all workers. This is particularly true for women who have been able to break through long-established barriers, get jobs in industry, and become members of industrial unions. These women are guaranteed wages equal to men in the same job categories — wages substantially higher on the average than those of the big majority of workers who are women.

New forces for the working class

The very workings of the world capitalist system that reinforce discrimination based on race, language, citizenship, and sex at the same time bring masses of new workers into the U.S. labor force — from Latin American and Asian immigrants escaping the unlivable conditions created by imperialism in their homelands, to women who must go to work to support their families, to members of farm families driven off the land here and abroad. The working class in the United States is being reinforced daily by the influx of more workers who are Black, Latino, or Asian; more workers who are immigrants; more workers who speak Spanish or another language other than English; more workers who are female.

These new legions of workers will be an increasing component of the working class. Today workers who are male and white are 47 percent of the work force. But the majority of new entrants into the work force are Black, Latino, Asian, and female. In little more than a decade, 85 percent of the new entrants into the labor force in the United States will be Black, Latino, Asian, or female.

IV. WHAT THE LABOR MOVEMENT MUST DO

These are the conditions facing working people in the United States and worldwide as we look ahead to the massive increase in joblessness and impoverishment that capitalism holds in store for us. How should the labor movement respond today to these facts in the new political situation opened by the inevitability of a depression and wrenching social crisis?

Strong enough to fight back and win

Despite the blows we have been dealt in the last few years, the employers and their government have not been able to take back the gains for democratic rights and equality of the last two decades that have strengthened the unity and potential fighting capacity of our class, the working class. In our struggles to defend our rights and living conditions advances *can* be made; defeats are *not* inevitable.

The Socialist Workers Party believes that the unions and other organizations of working people need to chart a course of action that will draw us together, help us recognize our common interests, and thus strengthen our ability to fight back and win. We don't have to start from scratch. We can build on struggles that have already begun to be waged by unions, Black and Chicano and other Latino organizations, women's rights groups, working farmers, and others among the oppressed and exploited in this country and around the world.

- We should join in the demand for a shorter workweek with no loss in pay that has been fought for by unions in South Korea, West Germany, and other countries. Only an international campaign by labor and our allies demanding action by governments worldwide can create the hundreds of millions of new jobs and lift the burden of capitalist-caused unemployment off the backs of working people.

• We should carry forward the battle that has been fought in the United States to overcome the race and sex discrimination used to divide working people on the job and throughout society. This fight to enforce affirmative action has begun to be waged in a number of countries and will more and more become an international campaign.

• And we should join in the fight that is already being waged by workers and rural toilers — from Brazil to Zimbabwe, from Cuba to Trinidad — to cancel the debt to the imperialist bankers that is ravaging the semicolonial world and threatening a financial catastrophe that will devastate working people worldwide.

These are demands for us all, demands that call for *action* by every organization that claims to speak for working people. These demands correspond to the immediate and ever-more burning need to provide us protection — today and as the crisis breaks over us.

Our starting point cannot be as "U.S." workers. Nor do we begin with the illusion that we can somehow protect "our own" jobs and let the devil take the hindmost. Only the devil will win!

Our fight encompasses the employed and the unemployed, from imperialist and semicolonial countries alike. Capitalism itself — through the world economic and social crisis it engenders — is driving more and more of us together to defend our interests as an international class.

A campaign for these pressing needs can unify workers around the world and give us the strength we need to win. It can increase our self-confidence and bring growing numbers into political action that points toward the struggle for a workers' and farmers' government.

The unions in the United States should take up these demands for a shorter workweek with no loss in pay, for affirmative action, and for cancellation of the debt. The labor movement should discuss them, explain them, campaign for them, and reach out to workers and workers' organizations around the world to begin building an international movement to win them.

Let's look more closely at these demands.

V. AN ACTION PROGRAM FOR THE WORKING CLASS

The most fundamental division among wage-workers is between the employed and the unemployed. This reflects the basic condition of competition among workers under capitalism — a social system in which our abilities are reduced by the employers to a commodity, *our labor power*, to be bought at the cheapest available price on the labor market. To cut costs and boost profits, the capitalists cold-bloodedly decide how many of us to replace with machines, and they become more and more resistant to improvements in wages and conditions on the job.

Today we already find ourselves divided in a hundred ways in the face of the grinding economic and social conditions we confront. And much worse times are coming.

The employers, as well as the politicians and newspaper editors who serve them, persistently try to get employed workers to look at unemployed workers as somehow not part of the working class. Those of us who are jobless are branded as "lazy," "shiftless," "dangerous," "welfare cheats," the "criminal class" and — most insistently — a threat to the jobs of others. Middle-class commentators who feign sympathy with our plight categorize us as the "poor," the "underclass," a "subclass," the "homeless" — anything and everything but what we are: workers who suffer the various conditions inflicted upon us by capitalism.

In the United States we are told to think of ourselves as "American" workers, with interests separate and apart from workers in other countries. The politicians of both big-business parties, from Daniel Moynihan and George Bush to Jesse Jackson and Michael Dukakis, say some form of protection for "U.S." industry is needed to protect "U.S." jobs. They urge us to join forces with the employers and their government in Washington to impose tariffs, quotas, or other aggressive, restrictive, and inflationary measures against imports of goods produced in other countries.

Some say they are for "free trade" but call for using U.S. government muscle to force other countries to open their doors to more exports from the United States, with various forms of retaliation proposed "if necessary."

AFL-CIO officials top everyone in vocal support for these trade barriers. To win working-class support for such measures, the labor officialdom even tries to play on our feelings of solidarity with fellow workers abroad, demagogically railing against U.S. companies that "export jobs" to semicolonial countries where "slave labor" is used. They urge us to demand that employers instead "invest in America" and create jobs for the unemployed.

At the same time, when it comes to South Africa — the one country whose labor movement and organizations such as the African National Congress are calling for worldwide economic sanctions — the capitalist politicians and most union officials have refused to push for a 100 percent boycott on trade and other links with the apartheid regime.

In advocating restrictive trade measures, labor officials are in fact supporting the bosses' profits and power, not defending our jobs or unity. They promote the reactionary myth that the only way to prevent layoffs and joblessness is to help big business in the United

States become more competitive and profitable. We are urged to be "more productive" and to collaborate with the owners of "our plant" and "our industry."

The ruling rich, the capitalist politicians, and the union bureaucrats all try to convince us that we are "Americans," not workers. And that the employers, too, are "Americans," not bosses. We are told that we have a common "national" interest with the employers that pits us against Japanese, British, Brazilian, Mexican, Angolan, and other "national" interests. We're supposed to support the employers' government, their political parties, and their foreign policy in order to defend "our" national interests.

This entire propaganda effort is designed to prevent us from seeing and acting on the fact that we have no common interests with those who grow wealthy off our labor and who are responsible for the deteriorating conditions under which we work and live. It is designed to keep us from recognizing that we are all part of an international class of workers who face a coming catastrophe as a result of the workings of the capitalist system. This propaganda plays on our fears and insecurities. It introduces and reinforces racist and nationalist prejudices.

Acceptance of these reactionary notions points in the opposite direction from the greater unity that workers must forge to become strong enough to fight and win.

The products that workers can produce are desperately needed by working people the world over, as are the housing, schools, hospitals, roads, bridges, and child-care centers that workers can build. Despite these social needs, however, the number of unemployed workers around the world right now runs into hundreds of millions. The International Labor Organization reports that in 1987 official unemployment in Latin America had increased for the seventh straight year. It currently stands at nearly 70 million out of a population of 421 million — the equivalent of more than 40 million unemployed in the United States! A similar devastation exists in Africa and Asia.

In the more economically developed capitalist countries, the jobless rate is at a historic high for nondepression years. According to government figures it is 20 percent in Spain, 15.6 percent in Italy, 14 percent in the Netherlands, 10.8 percent in Belgium, 10.3 percent in France, 8.8 percent in Britain, 8.9 percent in West Germany, 7.3 percent in New Zealand, and 7.9 percent in Australia. Japan boasts a jobless figure of less than 3 percent. But if you add in part-time workers seeking full-time work and workers so discouraged that they have given up looking for a job, then the figure jumps to more than 8 percent — the same as in the United States for comparable categories.

While millions are either out of work or underemployed, millions of others are forced to work overtime. The forty-hour workweek fought for by workers around the world and codified into federal law in the United States in 1938 is a fiction for the many workers who put in fifty-, sixty-, and seventy-hour weeks.

In addition, overtime, speedup, and reorganization of the work process have brutally increased the amount of labor we have to do. This intensification is leading to increased injuries, permanent disablement, and job-related deaths.

Jobs for all — shorten the workweek

Working people must join together in an international struggle to protect ourselves from growing unemployment. We must mount a campaign to fight for jobs for all — a worldwide campaign to radically reduce the workweek, with not a penny reduction in pay. If the workweek were shortened to thirty hours with forty-hours' pay, that would immediately open up the possibility of jobs for millions of workers. It would strengthen us to fight speedup on the job and to struggle for social programs to meet the needs of working people.

The fight for a shorter workweek must be a political fight directed at the federal government, not simply at each individual employer, plant by plant, industry by industry. We should demand:

- Legislation immediately establishing a maximum legal workweek of thirty hours and a working day of six hours.
- Government enforcement of this legislation through provisions making any work beyond six hours a day or thirty hours a week completely voluntary, and setting the minimum premium pay for overtime at double the hourly wage rate.
- A full forty-hours' pay for all government employees. The government itself, which legislates and enforces hours of work, must guarantee that the workers it employs take no loss in pay. A movement strong enough to win a thirty-hour workweek will lay a powerful basis for a struggle by labor to maintain a full forty-hours' pay for every worker in every factory, industry, and workplace, as well.

This fight for a thirty-hour week at forty-hours' pay can unite workers who are out of work, workers involuntarily pushed into part-time jobs, young workers who have never had a steady job, and workers forced to work overtime and victimized by speedup.

A shorter workweek would help lessen the increasing safety hazards in the workplace and the wear and tear on our minds, nerves, and muscles that accumulates day after day. It would give us more time to ourselves and to relax with families and friends and more energy to organize politically to fight for our rights.

When employers introduce new machinery and technology to intensify labor and boost profits, we, the producers, should not be the victims of our increasing productivity. We should not end up on the street with no job. This is yet another reason to mount a fight to reduce the workweek and spread the available work. Working people should benefit from new methods that have the potential to enable us to produce more with less labor.

The fight for adoption and enforcement of a thirty-hour workweek goes hand in hand with other demands on the government to provide a job for every working person:

• Put those of us without jobs to work restoring what capitalism has destroyed and building public facilities we desperately need. Housing, schools, and medical facilities are all deteriorating today. The railroads, air transport, subways, highways, bridges, and tunnels are all in life-threatening disrepair. Rivers and lakes are polluted, and poisonous waste dump sites dot the map.

The capitalist government has the responsibility and the resources to correct these conditions. We must demand that it launch a program of public works to give millions of workers productive jobs. Like other government employment, these jobs should have a thirty-hour week and forty-hours' pay.

An international effort to build desperately needed factories, production equipment, and social projects in the semicolonial countries would employ millions of workers.

• Provide unemployment benefits to workers for as long as we're out of work and no matter why we're out of work. Jobless benefits should be set at the level of the average union wage in manufacturing, not a pittance insufficient to get by on.

• Extend unemployment benefits to layers of jobless working people who are ineligible for unemployment compensation under current laws. These benefits should cover farmers who have been driven off the land by profit-hungry bankers. They must be extended to young workers who have been denied work since they began looking and to women who have just begun hunting for work but have not yet found a job.

An international fight

From the origins of the modern working class more than two centuries ago, struggles over the length of the workweek and the working day have been at the center of our battles against ruthless exploitation by the employing class. From the beginning, this struggle has spilled beyond national boundaries, as well. The shorter workweek is a demand that workers in every country can fight for. It is truly an international demand. It can be won through an international campaign.

The shorter workweek is our answer to quotas, tariffs, and other weapons of Wall Street's economic aggression. Trade barriers can never be an international demand of the working class. Workers in Japan will never be won to support calls for higher U.S. tariffs to restrict the import of cars. Workers in Argentina will never be won to the fight for European Common Market quotas limiting imports of beef into Western Europe.

Those of us who believe we can escape the impending depression by trying to save "our" jobs at the expense of workers here or abroad will find ourselves out in the street along with hundreds of millions of others. There is no strategy to negotiate "job security" for workers in any single plant, industry, union, or country. We can only advance the fight against unemployment by uniting with the victims around the world of the disaster capitalism is preparing.

Protecting our incomes against inflation

The price explosions of the 1970s and early 1980s showed us that the threat of accelerating inflation is very real as the economic crisis worsens. We will face massive unemployment *and* rising prices.

To deal with this problem of rising prices, some unions have won cost-of-living escalator clauses from various employers. Even these protections — which were rarely pegged to offset the true drop in buying power and covered only a small proportion of workers — have increasingly fallen under the fire of the employers' drive to force concessions out of us and drive down real wages. While more than 60 percent of unionized workers had cost-of-living clauses in their contracts in 1977, fewer than 40 percent still had such wage adjustments in 1987.

Working people are not responsible for inflation, any more than we're to blame for unemployment. Joblessness and rising prices result from the ceaseless competition for profits that is the heartbeat of the capitalist system.

To protect ourselves against the effects of these twin evils, the labor movement must campaign not only for a sliding scale of hours — the thirty-hour workweek at no loss in pay — but for a sliding scale of wages, as well.

- Demand that the government establish automatic cost-of-living adjustments in the wages for all public employees; pensions; and welfare, unemployment, and Social Security payments.
- Wage a fight for a sliding scale of wages — that is, full and automatic cost-of-living protection — in all union contracts and for

workers in every plant and workplace.

That's the only way to keep up with inflation.

Affirmative action quotas

As long as the employers can deny jobs to some workers because we are Black, Chicano, Puerto Rican, Asian, American Indian, foreign-born, or female, they can keep our class divided and weaken our ability to protect the jobs, wages, and working conditions of all workers. As we have shown by facts and figures, such discrimination is institutionalized in capitalist society. Moreover, the very way that capitalism operates day in and day out constantly reproduces and thus reinforces these inequalities, to the benefit of the employers. Left to their own devices, the capitalists will never enforce measures to insure equality on the job market and in the workplace. They will back every discriminatory practice inside the labor movement itself. We must demand that the government:

- Establish and enforce affirmative action quotas to achieve preferential hiring and upgrading of workers who are Black, Latino, or women.

The labor movement can combat the inequality that the bosses use to divide and weaken our class only by demanding such mandatory quotas. Under capitalism, "voluntary affirmative action" is a contradiction in terms.

Affirmative action applies not only in the job market and in the workplace. We must also demand that the government:

- Enforce quotas to guarantee that Blacks and other victims of race and national discrimination be given preference in college admission, loans, and housing.
- Enforce busing to desegregate schools in order to provide equal educational opportunities to students who are Black or Latino.

Special measures are also needed to overcome sex divisions in the working class. Most importantly, we need to fight to tear down the employment barriers of sex segregation that block women from the only jobs that can raise the value of their labor power over time and close the income gap with men. We must demand:

- Quotas for hiring women into industrial jobs, as well as preferential training and upgrading in the workplace. Only in this way can women's powerful numbers be brought into the industrial unions. Only in this way will the average pay of working women begin to be raised, boosting the wage level for the entire working class.

The discrimination against women by educational institutions, banks, and housing authorities is taking a greater and greater toll as more and more women find themselves responsible for the support of families. The labor movement must fight to:

- Enforce affirmative action for women in education, housing, and loans, as well as in employment and on the job.

Affirmative action measures are especially needed to defend the unity of the working class when large-scale layoffs begin. Otherwise workers hired through affirmative action programs are more likely to be laid off than other workers, deepening divisions in the working class at the very moment when our unity and thus fighting capacity is most needed. To counter this sapping of labor's strength, the unions must wage a fight to:

- Structure the seniority system in such a way that when layoffs hit, the percentage of workers who are Black, Latino, and female does not decline. Past gains in hiring and upgrading must not be permitted to erode during recessions. Otherwise, every step toward equality will turn out to be a cruel illusion.

Raise the minimum wage

A disproportionate number of those working at minimum wage are young, Black, Latino, or female. The employing class, through oppression and prejudice, has kept the price of the labor power of these workers lower than that of the class as a whole.

In capitalist society wages are set from the bottom up, not the top down. In other words, what the bosses can get away with paying those of us who are worst-off sets the floor for what they'll get away with paying all the rest of us.

Affirmative action is needed to combat widening wage inequality, as well. A victorious fight for jobs and a living income can be conducted only through a broad social struggle that aims to raise the living standards and secure equal rights for those of us who are the most oppressed under capitalism. It is along that road that we can transform the labor movement into a social movement that will better the conditions of us all.

- Raise the federal minimum wage. For more than seven years the minimum wage as set by Congress has been a scrooge-like $3.35 an hour. This is the longest period without an increase since a minimum wage law was won in 1938. Taking account of inflation over that period, the current level has less buying power than thirty years ago! It is about one-third the average manufacturing wage, the lowest percentage ever.

Raising the minimum wage would help increase the wage level for all working people, particularly benefiting those who are the lowest paid. This would increase the unity and political strength of the working class.

Cancel the Third World debt

Unifying workers around the world also requires a fight to alter the unequal economic and social relations that perpetuate the oppression of the semicolonial nations by the ruling capitalist families of the United States, Canada, Western Europe, Japan, Australia, New Zealand, Israel, and South Africa.

The labor movement should call on Washington and the other imperialist governments to:

- Cancel the debt owed by the semicolonial countries.
- Eliminate all measures used to maintain unequal trade relations.
- Stop the dumping of goods on the world market at prices set to undercut sales by producers in semicolonial countries.
- Reestablish normal diplomatic and trade relations with all countries that have inherited a semicolonial economic structure from imperialist domination. This should include Cuba, Vietnam, Iran, Nicaragua, Libya, and North Korea.
- Resume foreign aid to Nicaragua, which has been ravaged by seven years of Washington's contra war. Tens of thousands of Nicaraguan workers and peasants have been maimed and had their homes and farms destroyed. They continue to face shortages of food and other essential items. The U.S. government should provide the people of Nicaragua with construction materials, medicines, food, farm implements, and other badly needed supplies.
- Support the development of barter — that is exchanges that don't require hard currency — and other mutually advantageous trade agreements among the semicolonial countries.
- End all restrictions on trade union rights throughout the world.
- Abolish all restrictions on immigrant workers — regardless of citizenship — that reduce them to second-class status with less than equal protection under the law.
- Abolish all restrictions on travel between countries so that working people are free to seek work wherever we want and to hold meetings and discussions, as well as engage in other political activity, with fellow workers in other countries.

* * *

The creeping social crisis that has been devastating broad layers of working people and regions of the world has driven some of us to the point of giving up hope. The pressures will mount still further with the worldwide depression and generalized social crisis that lies ahead.

But an international movement for a shorter workweek to provide jobs for all, affirmative action quotas aimed at achieving real equality, and cancellation of the Third World debt can convince hundreds of millions of workers and farmers worldwide that now is the time to take up the fight.

By championing these demands, the labor movement in the United States will be joining in a campaign that has already been launched by working people in Africa, Asia, and Latin America for what they have called a "new international economic order."

Through such a campaign, each and every one of us has the potential to recognize not only our strength as part of a united movement of working people, but also our individual worth as human beings with the capacity to think and to act. Working people the world over will discover that we are not only the ones who suffer under capitalism, but are at the same time the ones capable of waging a united and victorious fight to change the world.

These proposals should be taken up by workers' organizations in the United States and around the world. They should be discussed, explained, and circulated as widely as possible in organizations of working people and the oppressed.

This fighting perspective can unite working people in a worldwide movement to defend our most immediate interests today. It does so with a clear view to the much bigger battles that will confront us with the onset of the economic catastrophe that capitalism is bringing tomorrow — battles that we are convinced will lead toward the fight for socialism.

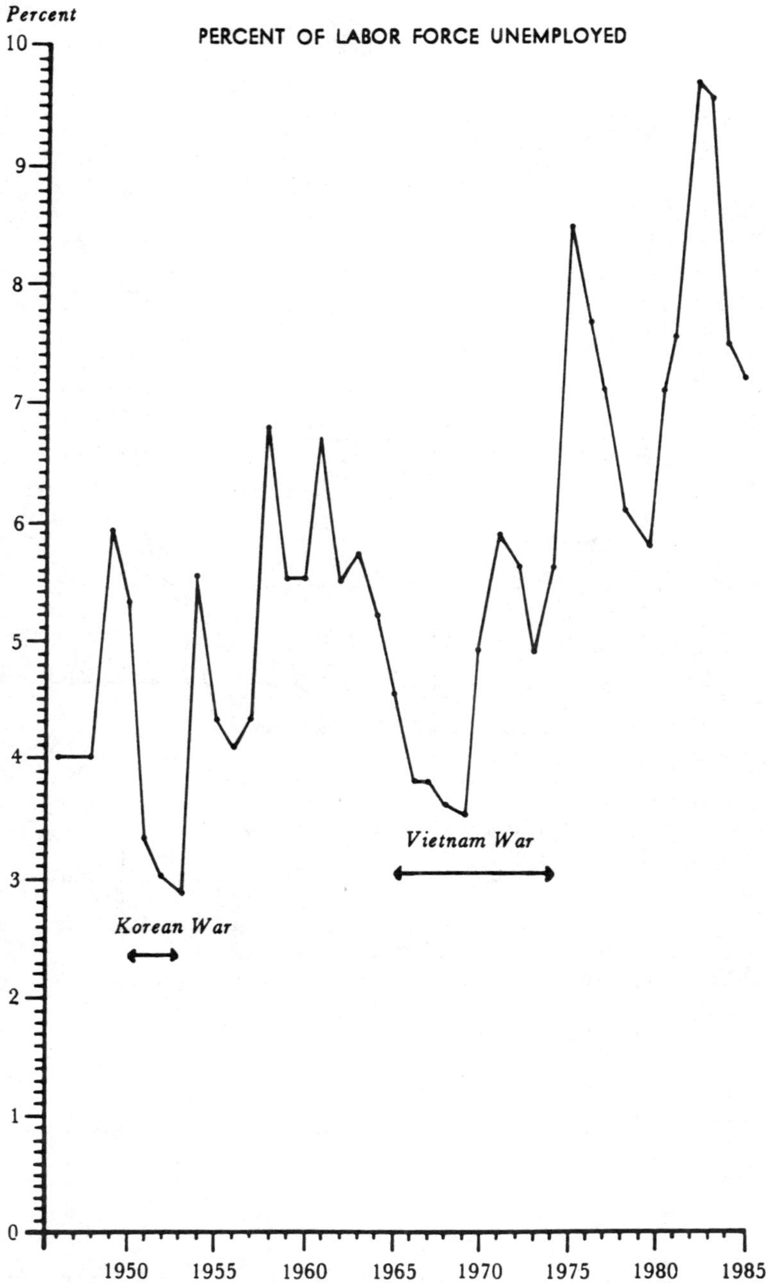

Washington is crowing that jobless rate today is *only* 5.6 percent. But that represents almost seven million workers, and is higher than most years between 1941 and 1975. Plus, millions are not counted in official unemployment statistics. For working people who are Black, unemployment is more than 12 percent; for Black youth, 35 percent.

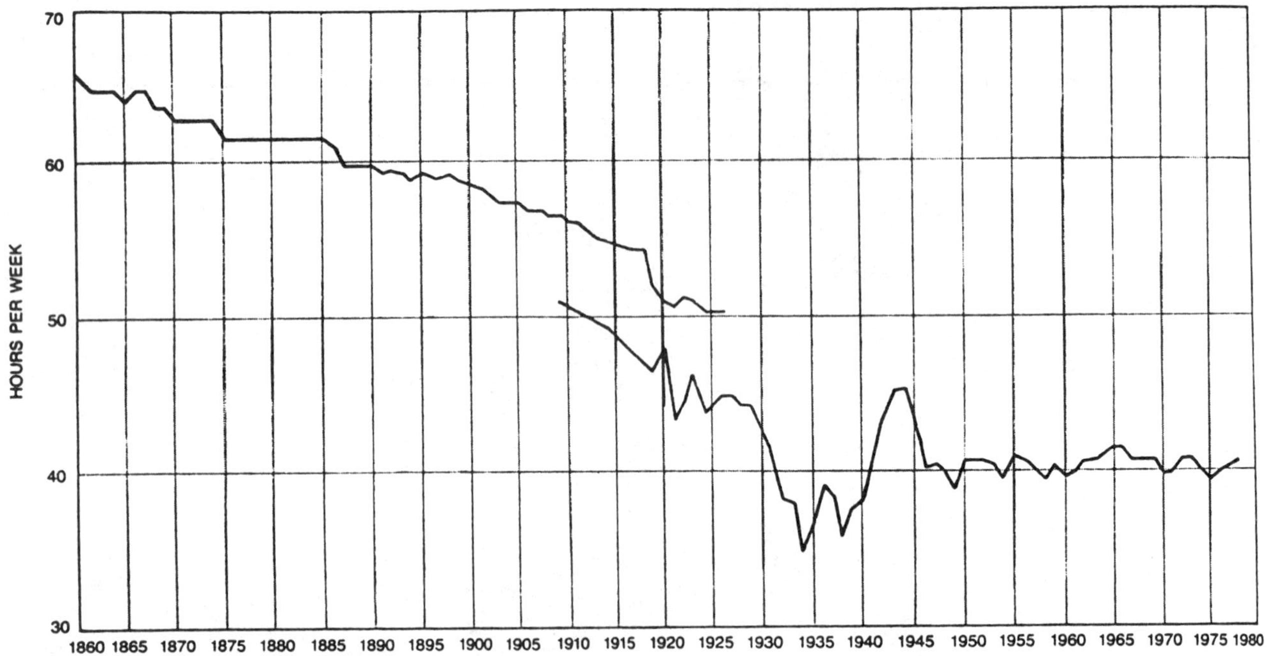

Workweek in manufacturing industries in United States. Struggles to shorten workweek have led to decline from sixty-seven hours in 1860 to about forty-two in 1950. Since then it has remained about the same. The legal forty-hour workweek is a myth for many workers in the United States, who put in fifty-, sixty-, and seventy-hour weeks. In many other countries, the average hours worked are even longer. Thus, while millions are out of work or underemployed, millions of others are forced to work overtime. The discontinuity in the curve, over the period 1910 through 1925, reflects a change in how statistics were made involving principally changes in the accounting of the time of part-time and seasonal workers.

The Fight for a Shorter Workweek, Yesterday and Today

by Doug Jenness

The following article is based on columns originally published in the June 24 and July 1, 1988, issues of the socialist newsweekly, the Militant.

Usually when a writer or speaker reels off a lot of statistics, they can be pretty hard to follow and the main point gets lost. But when those figures are put in a visual form the impact can be striking. The chart on page 26 of this pamphlet is a case in point.

Two things immediately hit you when you study how the average number of hours in the workweek of manufacturing workers in the United States has changed in the last 130 years.

The first is that there was a relatively steady decline between 1860 and the late 1940s — with the exception of the World War II years when pressure by the government, employers, and labor officialdom to produce for their war effort drove up the average workweek.

The second is that for the last forty years the average workweek has hovered around forty hours. According to the chart this is the longest period without a substantial reduction in 130 years.

The reduction in the average numbers of hours a week didn't occur automatically, as part of the laws of capitalist development. Nor did the employers suddenly get an attack of goodwill and lower the workweek voluntarily.

It took a long, hard-fought struggle by several generations of workers around the world. The fight to lower the average number of hours in the workweek was a central part of the struggle to overcome the deepest division within the working class — that between the employed and the unemployed. This division is among the employers' most powerful weapons in blocking the development of a strong and united workers' movement. A shorter workweek both opens up many new jobs for the unemployed and at the same time makes it easier for employed workers to fight brutal speedup and degradation of working conditions by the bosses.

Fight for the ten-hour day

When industrial capitalism first emerged and machinery began to be employed on a significant scale late in the eighteenth century, the capitalists pushed to extend the number of hours workers worked. Working days of fourteen and sixteen hours became common.

It was inevitable that the employers would do this. Once the working class had produced enough value to replace the plant and equipment used up and to cover the costs of their own labor power — that is enough to live on and feed, clothe, and train a new generation of wage workers — every hour worked creates profits for the employer.

One of the first actions of the working class as it began to organize itself was to fight to shorten the workday. The first significant struggle around this was the ten-hour-day movement that emerged in Britain, the United States, and other industrializing countries in the 1820s and gathered steam in the next couple of decades. In the United States, working-class organizations formed committees to fight for this. Scores of strikes were organized to press for this demand. Meetings, petitions, and other forms of activity were part of the campaign.

The fight won results.

In 1840, President Martin Van Buren issued an executive order setting the workday for public employees at ten hours, with no reduction in pay. In 1847, New Hampshire became the first state to legislate the ten-hour day and by the 1860s this had become standard for most states.

In Britain, legislation setting the workday at ten hours was adopted by parliament in 1847.

Of course, getting this demand incorporated into law didn't make it a fact. Workers continued to have to fight to force the employers to abide by the law. Even so, the result was that the average working day in the United States went from 12.5 hours in 1830 to 11 in 1860.

Impetus from revolutionary defeat of chattel slavery

The ten-hour day movement was followed by the fight for an eight-hour day. After the U.S. Civil War (1861-1865) — and to a significant degree under the impetus of the victorious revolution that swept away chattel slavery — there was a new rise in the labor movement both in the United States and Europe.

"In the United States of America," Karl Marx wrote in *Capital*, "every independent workers' movement was paralyzed as long as slavery disfigured a part of the republic. Labor in a white skin cannot emancipate itself where it is branded in a black skin. However, a new life immediately rose from the death of slavery. The first fruit of the American Civil War was the eight hours' agitation, which ran from the Atlantic to the Pacific, from New England to California, with the seven-league boots of a locomotive."

From 1866, when the eight-hour day was proposed by the National Labor Union, until well into this century, this became a major demand of the labor movement. And it was not always a peaceful fight. A good many workers lost their lives as a result of police attacks on demonstrations and strikes demanding the eight-hour day.

It also became an international fight as workers' organizations in many countries became part of the campaign. When the American Federation of Labor called for international demonstrations on May 1, 1890, demanding the eight-hour day, the labor and socialist organizations in many countries responded and tens of thousands of workers participated. This was the origins of May Day, the international working-class holiday celebrated each year in most countries.

"One army under one flag"

Frederick Engels, the foremost communist leader at the time, noted the importance of these actions for the development of international unity among working people. The workers, he said, "mobilized for the first time as One army, under One flag, and fighting for One immediate aim: an eight-hour working day. . . . The spectacle we are now witnessing will make the capitalists and landowners of all lands realize that today the proletarians are, in very truth, united."

Few workers today have any living memory of the fight to reduce the working day. This is an important part of the historical experience of the working class that deserves study. But we should do so with the recognition that there's not going to be any repeat of the ten-hour- or eight-hour-day movements.

That's not to say that there won't be an international fight to reduce the working day. There definitely will be. But it will occur in a very different world context and stage of capitalism.

Does history "repeat itself"?

"History repeats itself." That's virtually a household maxim. But like so many expressions of this sort, it's not true. Human society can't turn the clock back and rerun a chunk of life any more than individuals can.

Does that mean that learning lessons from history has no value for today? No. But it does mean that experiences from the past can't be copied to resolve today's problems or those that are coming.

For example, studying the labor upsurge of the 1930s in the United States, which led to the rise of the Congress of Industrial Organizations (CIO), can't give us the concrete answers to how to lead a strike or rejuvenate a campaign of the labor movement today. No account of the CIO has been written that can serve as a how-to book for today or the future, nor can one be written.

But what is very useful about seriously studying past experiences of working people is that they can give us an understanding of how opportunities and obstacles were met, what the conquests are that we stand on, and what limits we still face in our struggle against oppression and exploitation. It helps hone the tool that our brain is, enabling us to learn more from experiences and make more effective decisions. This, in turn, makes us more effective political thinkers.

What, then, can we learn from the struggles of earlier generations of workers who fought to shorten the workday to ten hours and then to eight hours?

Lessons from earlier battles

Above all we can see that the employers were unable to keep lengthening the working day and imposing speedup and other dehumanizing conditions without resistance from workers.

But the ten-hour- and eight-hour-day movements can't be repeated. Many things were different in the 1820s through the 1850s, for example, when the fight for the ten-hour day was strongest.

The struggle for the ten-hour day went hand in hand with the first steps by workers to organize themselves. Factory workers were still a relatively small portion of the population in almost every country, and the fledgling labor organizations were based mainly among workers in the skilled trades.

The movement was also connected with, and spurred on by, the workers' fight to knock down property qualifications and restrictions based on religion for voting and holding office.

Moreover, in the United States there were still vast unsettled lands and a major demand of working people was for the government to grant land to those willing to farm it.

Labor in a black skin remained in chains throughout the South. The ten-hour-day movement in the United States coincided with and shared many activists with the struggle to abolish slavery and indentured servitude.

The world context was also different from today. The ten-hour-day movement in the United States was part of a struggle in Britain and a few other countries, but it was far from being worldwide. Most of the world had not yet been drawn into domination by capitalist economic relations. The opportunities for the capitalist exploiters to get out of crises by expanding into new parts of the world was in sharp contrast with their situation today.

The eight-hour-day movement, which emerged after the victory over the slaveholders in the U.S. Civil War and continued into the twentieth century, was connected to the fight of industrial workers to organize unions. It also coincided with the rise of the modern imperialist system and the continued opportunities by the capitalist rulers for expansion.

It became far more of an international movement than the earlier struggle for a shorter workweek, but for the most part the struggles of colonial peoples and of workers in the imperialist countries were not integrated.

The fight in today's world

The rise of a new struggle for a shorter workweek will emerge under very different conditions. It's going to be part of working people's fight throughout the world to defend ourselves from the economic crises that already confront growing layers of us and from the even more disastrous consequences of the coming depression.

As tens of millions are thrown out of work the necessity of uniting in a fight to protect ourselves will pose ever more sharply the need for reducing the workweek and spreading the available jobs to more workers.

The fight for shortening the workweek will be intertwined with the struggle to prevent our incomes from being drastically slashed as a result of inflation.

This fight cannot win without being linked to the struggle for affirmative action quotas in hiring, education, and on the job for Blacks, Chicanos, Puerto Ricans, Asian-Americans, immigrant workers, and women. The battle to overcome the effects of discrimination and inequality is necessary in order to unite the working class in an effective fight for jobs and a living income.

An international campaign by working people for a shorter workweek will also be inseparable from the fight of Third World peoples against the worsening conditions resulting from the debt squeeze of the big bankers in New York, London, Paris, and the other financial centers. It will join together with struggles by farmers facing deepening indebtedness and dispossession from the land almost everywhere.

The capitalist world today is far more interdependent and interconnected than ever before. This was shown by the speed with which the Wall Street crash in October 1987 spread to stock markets around the world. This has created the basis and the necessity for greater unity by working people in both the imperialist countries and the semicolonial world. Workers in the Soviet Union and Eastern Europe will also be drawn into this international battle, as the bureaucratic misleaders of those workers' states increasingly resort to capitalist methods in the face of the deepening crisis of their regimes.

The capitalist rulers have no foreseeable road out of the coming depression and social crisis — neither colonization of new continents, opening of new lands, creation of massive new markets, or even armed conflicts to redivide the world among themselves.

This means that in defending ourselves against the ravages of the coming economic disaster, the stakes will be high. And this defensive struggle will inevitably pass over to a struggle by working people to remove capitalist political rule and establish our own power — a government of the workers and exploited farmers.

Cuban Leaders Speak Out

Che Guevara and the Cuban Revolution
Writings and Speeches of Ernesto Che Guevara
Describes Cuba's revolutionary war, its efforts to overcome economic backwardness, the task of developing a new social consciousness in the transition to socialism, and Cuba's commitment to freedom struggles throughout the world. 413 pp., $11.95.

Fidel Castro Speeches
Cuba's Internationalist Foreign Policy 1975–80.
Topics include solidarity with Angola, Ethiopia, Vietnam, and Nicaragua; Cuba's policy of providing teachers, doctors, and other personnel wherever requested; and U.S.-Cuban relations. 391 pp., $9.95.

Fidel Castro Speeches, Volume 2
Building Socialism in Cuba, 1960–82
Describes efforts by the Cuban government and Communist Party to involve working people in making fundamental decisions that affect their lives and to combat the rise of privilege and bureaucratism. 368 pp., $9.95

Fidel Castro Speeches 1984-85
War and Crisis in the Americas
Speeches and interviews focusing on Latin America's escalating social crisis, why its foreign debt cannot be paid and must be cancelled, and the need for solidarity with Nicaragua. 268 pp., $9.95.

Nothing Can Stop the Course of History
by Fidel Castro as interviewed by
Jeffrey M. Elliot and Mervyn M. Dymally
Discusses U.S.-Cuban relations, Cuba's involvement in the fight against apartheid rule in southern Africa, the overthrow of the Grenada revolution, and Latin America's foreign debt. 276 pp., $8.95.

Socialism and Man in Cuba
by Ernesto Che Guevara
Takes up the major challenges faced in the transition to socialism. Includes Fidel Castro's speech on the twentieth anniversary of Guevara's death. 37 pp., $1.95.

Available from Pathfinder. See inside front cover for addresses.

by Malcolm X

The Autobiography of Malcolm X
460 pp., $3.50

By Any Means Necesary
184 pp., $7.95

Malcolm X on Afro-American History
74 pp., $4.95

Malcolm X Speaks
226 pp., $6.95

Malcolm X Talks to Young People
Pamphlet, 32 pp., $.75

Two Speeches by Malcolm X
Pamphlet, 32 pp., $1.00

Available from Pathfinder. See inside front cover for addresses.

New International

A Magazine of Marxist Politics and Theory

No. 1 (Fall 1983) $4
Their Trotsky and Ours: Communist Continuity Today
by Jack Barnes
Lenin and the Colonial Question
by Carlos Rafael Rodríguez

No. 2 (Winter 1983-84) $4
The Working-Class Road to Peace
by Brian Grogan
The Social Roots of Opportunism
by Gregory Zinoviev

No. 3 (Spring-Summer 1984) $4
The Workers' and Farmers' Government: A Popular Revolutionary Dictatorship
by Mary-Alice Waters
The FSLN and the Nicaraguan Revolution
by Tomás Borge

No. 4 (Spring 1985) $4
The Worker-Farmer Alliance in the U.S.
articles by Jack Barnes and Doug Jenness
Revolutionary Perspectives and Leninist Continuity in the U.S.
resolution of the Socialist Workers Party

No. 5 (Fall 1985) $5
The Coming Revolution in South Africa
by Jack Barnes
The Future Belongs to the Majority
by Oliver Tambo

No. 6 (1987) $6.50
The Second Assassination of Maurice Bishop
by Steve Clark
Cuba: A Historic Moment
by Fidel Castro
Washington's Fifty-Year Domestic Contra Operation
by Larry Seigle

Available from Pathfinder. See inside front cover for addresses.